INVASIVE COLOR

INVASIVE CoLoR

Using Invasive Species as Natural Dyes

THERESA MARIE HORNSTEIN

Hezzie Mae
BOOK PUBLISHING

Duluth, Minnesota

Copyright © 2025 by Theresa Hornstein

REL Print Group, a Hezzie Mae Publication
Duluth, MN.
www.HezzieMae.com

All rights reserved. Hezzie Mae supports copyright. Copyright fuels creativity, encourages diverse voices, promotes free speech, and creates a vibrant culture. Thank you for complying with copyright laws by not reproducing, scanning, or distributing any part of this book in any form without permission from the publisher.

ISBN: 979-8-9911532-8-7

Cover and Interior Design by Hailee Pavey of Pavey Design
www.paveydesign.com

DEDICATION

I would like to dedicate this book to all the people who helped me. Without you, this would not have been possible.

To my children—Katrina, Nikoli, and Elyse—who put up with many years of strange things brewing on the stove and skeins of yarn scattered everywhere.

To my fiber friends: Jody, who continually encouraged me and has ideas for further editions; Maria, who is always up for going collecting; and Lisa, who keeps me experimenting.

To Heather and Hailee—who brought my project to print.

CONTENTS

11	Preface	
13	What is an Invasive Species?	
17	Basic Safety Measures	
	19	Safety Steps
21	The Dye Process	
	21	Things That Influence the Dye Process
	22	Equipment
	23	Fiber Types
	26	Mordants & Modifiers
	31	Methods
35	How to Use This Book	
36	Notes Space	

(Contents Continued on Next Page)

7

CONTENTS *(Continued)*

- **40** — Amur maple (*Acer ginnala*)
- **42** — Big-leaf lupine (*Lupinus polyphyllus*)
- **44** — Birdsfoot trefoil (*Lotus corniculatus*)
- **46** — Bradford pear (*Pyrus calleryana*)
- **48** — Buckthorn
  — Common (*Rhamnus cathartica*)
  — Glossy (*Frangula alnus*)
- **52** — Notes Space
- **54** — Creeping bellflower (*Campanula rapunculoides*)
- **56** — Creeping Charlie (*Glechoma hederacea*)
- **58** — Curly dock (*Rhumex crispus*)
- **60** — Cutleaf teasel (*Dipsacus laciniatus*)
- **62** — Japanese knotweed (*Reynoutria japonica*)
- **64** — Notes Space

CONTENTS *(Continued)*

- **66** Mullein (Verbascum thapsus)
- **68** Norway maple (Acer platanoides)
- **70** Orange hawkweed (Hieracium aurantiacum)
- **72** Purple loosestrife (Lythrum salicaria)
- **74** Queen Anne's lace (Daucus carota)
- **76** Notes Space
- **78** Siberian Peashrub (Caragana arborescens)
- **80** Spotted knapweed (Centaurea stoebe ssp. Micranthos)
- **82** Tansy (Tanacetum vulgare)
- **84** Woad (Isatis tinctoria)
- **88** Wormwood (Artemisia absinthium)
- **90** Notes Space
- **92** About the Author

PREFACE

My exploration into using invasive species as natural dyes began upside down in a snowy hole with my snowshoes hung up in a thorny shrub. After nearly an hour of grabbing branches and slowly inching upward, I managed to pull myself out. But my undyed mittens were stained gold, and I could not get them to wash out. This was my introduction to buckthorn, and it started a 30-year adventure into the colors produced by invasive species.

In general, humans love color. People of every culture across time have decorated their homes, their furnishings, and themselves with color. Archeological digs have produced artifacts demonstrating that our ancestors enjoyed color and had a deep understanding of the chemistry of natural dyes and pigments. The source of their colors came from plants and minerals. Modern science is just now beginning to understand the chemistry behind some of the colors. However, natural dyes are highly variable; time of year, growing conditions, and even variation in the water used can modify the colors obtained.

The introduction of synthetic dyes in the mid-1800s replaced many of the natural dyes. These synthetics were based on coal tar rather than plants. Synthetic dyes had the advantage of producing consistent results. They were not dependent on seasonality, locale, or water quality. A dyer could get any color any time of year with synthetic dyes. Some of the earliest synthetic dyes were purples and reds, both colors difficult to obtain from natural dyes. The time-consuming and less consistent natural dyes fell out of favor, and much of the knowledge was forgotten.

In recent years, artisans have rediscovered natural dyes. Antique books containing recipes have been dusted off, and older terminology is being translated into modern language. Blue vitriol from the old texts is now known as copper sulfate; green vitriol is ferrous sulfate. While many of the dye recipes have been forgotten, modern analytical techniques are helping to rediscover historic natural dyes. In addition, modern dyers' experimentation adds to the knowledge base. One of the great pleasures of working with natural dyes is the joy of discovery—getting color from unexpected sources or new colors from altering techniques. Use the information in this book as a guide. The idea is to give a foundation in basic dye techniques and some examples. Feel free to experiment. Try new plants. Test out a new technique. Who knows what you will create!

WHAT IS AN INVASIVE SPECIES?

There are two primary criteria used to identify something as an invasive species. First, the organism cannot be native to the area. Many non-native species were introduced for a specific purpose. Perhaps they were beautiful plants introduced for landscaping or a new food crop brought in from its original home territory. Some were brought as sources of medicine, grazing for livestock, or economic purposes. Others come by accident, hitching rides in ballast tanks, stuck in shoe treads, or hidden in packing materials. Once in their new "home," these organisms can establish reproducing populations. These populations lack their natural predators and other control mechanisms of their home ecosystem and can begin to multiply almost uncontrollably.

Not all non-native species, even those that develop reproducing populations, count as invasive species. The second criterion is the harm the organism causes in its new environment. That harm can come in a variety of forms. Many invasives have massive reproductive potential. As their numbers increase, they begin to displace native species and disrupt the natural ecosystem. Disease-causing organisms have new hosts that lack an innate immunity to the organism. Others can disrupt the social or economic structure of an area. Ranchers can lose grazing land when plants like teasel invade. Waterfowl populations can be harmed when purple loosestrife crowds out their native food sources. Many of these organisms create large monocultures, squeezing out the other organisms in the region.

To complicate issues, various other terms and legal classifications are involved. For example, domesticated animals and plants under human control are not considered invasive species. Non-native means the organism has not been found in that area before. This is a broad category. It includes organisms from completely different continents, such as Japanese knotweed, which was brought to North America and Europe from its native Asia. However, it can also represent a population expanding into new ranges, such as plants moving north in response to climate change. A noxious weed is a plant that causes harm. It can be native or non-native. Many places have laws governing the removal, sale, and transportation of noxious weeds. Prohibited noxious weeds must be removed or controlled, and transporting parts of these organisms capable of reproducing, such as seeds or cuttings, is usually illegal.

Most states have lists of what is considered an invasive species in that state. These can usually be found in departments of natural resources or agriculture. Each state and province is slightly different. There are also legalities related to transporting and possessing invasive species. The specifics can usually be found under the same agency identifying the species. Always check.

Removing or controlling invasive plant species can be done in a number of ways.

 The best method is to prevent the introduction of a species. Before ordering seeds or plants, check to make sure they are not listed as invasive or regulated in the area where the plant will be grown. Avoid accidentally introducing organisms through seeds stuck to clothing or equipment.

 Removing flower heads before seed set through hand picking or mowing helps to prevent plants from spreading. This works best with annual and biennial plants. Perennials will usually regrow from the roots.

Digging or pulling out plants is another method. Many communities organize events, like buckthorn pulls, to remove the plants. However, root fragments can often be missed, especially with deep root systems, and can regrow, so it may take several years of repeated digging to get them all. Do not compost the plants that were removed. They will happily reestablish themselves in compost piles. Check with local agencies for their disposal recommendations.

 For large areas, controlled burns under permitted conditions can kill above-ground growth. This usually won't kill root systems. Large controlled burns are best handled by professionals.

 Biological controls have been used successfully on some species, but again, this is for the professionals. Biological controls are most often insects that feed only on a specific plant. They are introduced species, and there is always a risk of the organism changing food sources and becoming invasive. Years of research go into choosing biological controls.

 Herbicides can be used to eradicate invasive species, but this is best done by professionals. Most herbicides should be used with specialized equipment such as respirators, sprayers, and gloves, and it can be difficult to control the application. They are rarely used near water to prevent contamination of lakes and streams.

Dyeing requires roughly an equal weight of plant to the weight of fiber to be dyed. To achieve deep colors requires even more. While dyeing isn't going to solve the problem of invasive species, it can at least make a tiny dent in your local area. Do not feel guilty stripping the bark off a living tree or pulling all the flowers off several plants when working with an invasive species to produce beautiful yarns. When using an invasive species as a dye, it is guilt-free. Removing the plants is a service to the local ecosystem. An added benefit is the production of something beautiful.

BASIC SAFETY MEASURES

Safety needs to be taken into account when using natural dyeing. Natural does not equate with harmless. While not actually poisonous, some plants produce irritants, triggering allergic reactions or causing contact dermatitis, an itchy rash, or blisters. Others produce unpleasant effects if ingested. Some plants actually produce deadly toxins. Poison hemlock (Conium maculatum) is an herbaceous plant that can easily be confused with Queen Anne's lace (Daucus carota). The alkaloid toxin found in the hemlock plant attacks the nervous system and causes seizures and respiratory failure. Before collecting it, consider a plant's identity and any associated risks. Do not use toxic or irritating plants as dyes for safety's sake.

Always take personal safety precautions when harvesting dye plants. Maps or GPS apps reduce the risk of getting lost and can identify property ownership to prevent trespassing. Know the terrain in the harvest area. Are there risks—unstable ground, poisonous snakes, aggressive wildlife? Even the plants themselves can create a risk. The monocultures created by invasive species are often so dense that they can hide holes or deep water. Some plants, like teasel and buckthorn, come armed with spikes, so heavy leather gloves and protective clothing are a good idea.

Chemicals like washing soda, alum, and citric acid, used in the dye processes, have safe household uses but can be harmful if ingested or if they come into contact with skin or eyes. Powdered chemicals create an inhalation risk and may require the use of a mask. Good ventilation is essential. Many of the mordants (used to improve the permanence of natural dyes) and modifiers (used to alter the color) can pose their own risks. Toxic metals such as arsenic, lead, and chrome have been used as modifiers. Modern dyers rarely use them because of their toxicity, but they are listed in older dye recipes. Avoid using them. They are considered hazardous and require specialized disposal. However, even relatively safe chemicals, like iron or ammonia, can cause irritation on contact with the skin. For safety's sake, it is best to treat all substances used in dyeing as potential threats and use proper precautions—eye protection, water-proof gloves, aprons, and respiratory protection.

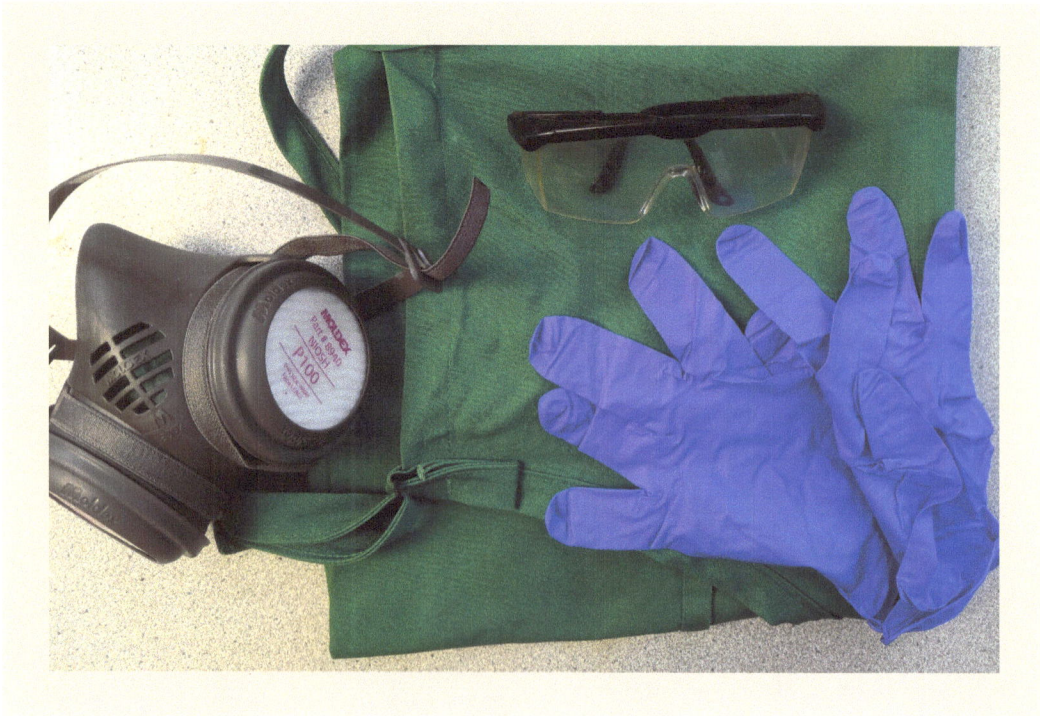

SAFETY STEPS

THESE SIMPLE RULES WILL HELP TO MAKE THE DYEING EXPERIENCE SAFER.

1 **Use gloves, goggles, and a water-resistant apron.** Waterproof gloves are a good idea both to minimize direct contact with the dye material and to keep from dyeing the skin and nails. Goggles protect the eyes from the inevitable splashing. An apron can provide some protection if the dye bath spills.

2 **Label all mordants and modifiers clearly.** Their packaging will usually be labeled with any specific safety issues and emergency treatment for contact. If the chemicals come with MSDS sheets, attach the sheet to the storage container. When not in use, store dye chemicals out of reach of children and pets.

3 **Keep your dye equipment separate from equipment that will come in contact with food.** Use different cutting boards, measuring tools, pots, and stirrers. Label them clearly as for dyeing only. Wash up the dye equipment with its own dedicated sponge. Store the dye equipment in a dedicated and clearly labeled box away from the kitchen when finished.

(Safety steps 4–7 continued on next page.)

(SIMPLE DYEING RULES CONTINUED)

4 **Never cook and dye at the same time.** Ideally, dyers work in a designated area or dye shed, but most small-scale dyers do not have that luxury. They work in their kitchens. Dyeing is a slow process, so it is tempting to have dye pots and food pots cooking at the same time. **Don't.** There is too much risk of grabbing the wrong spoon to stir or otherwise contaminating the food.

5 **Choose the materials wisely.** I have a personal rule of only using the safest materials. Chrome mordant produces some beautiful colors, but it is risky to work with and hard to dispose of safely. Make sure the plant material does not produce toxins or irritants.

6 **Work in a well-ventilated area.** Heating the dyes can release unpleasant fumes. Ammonia and vinegar are used as modifiers. Both release irritating fumes, especially when heated.

7 **Clean up carefully.** Use dedicated towels for cleaning up, or use paper towels. Wipe down all counters and tables well to make sure no dye materials are left. Scrub pots and other equipment well before storing.

THE DYE PROCESS

Things That Influence the Dye Process

Dyeing is very much a blending of art and science. Just as a painter knows different brushes produce different effects, and a potter knows different locations within the kiln can affect the glaze, many different factors can influence the final results of a dye pot. If you want the exact same results every time you dye, natural dyes are probably not for you. The concentration of dyes in a plant can vary yearly and from location to location. Different soils have different levels of nutrients and may produce different colors. Changes during the growing season may also alter the colors. For example, early-season leaves produce slightly different colors than late-season leaves.

Variations in water chemistry will impact the final color outcome when using natural dyes. City water differs chemically from well water and salt water from fresh. Bog water is acidic and rich in tannins. It produces different results than water without tannins. Both of the samples below were dyed using buckthorn berries picked on the same day from the same plant and dyed in the same pot. The yarns are both merino. One was dyed at a workshop in the northern part of the state and turned green. The other was dyed the next day at a workshop in the southern part of the state and turned yellow.

One way around the differences in water chemistry is to use distilled water, which can become expensive. If a quantity of yarn in the same color is needed for a project, it works best to dye it all at once in a single batch. If it need not match perfectly, embrace the variation.

Equipment

Dye work can be done with fairly simple tools. At the simplest levels, a pot, a heat source, something to stir with, and the safety equipment will suffice. Specific techniques (discussed later) use additional tools.

The choice of pot is important. The best dye pots are stainless steel, enamelware, ceramic, or glass. They are non-reactive and do not contribute to the dye reactions. Pots made of other metals can influence the final color by leaching metal ions into the dye bath. This can be taken advantage of with the pot acting as a mordant or a modifier. Cast iron leaches iron into the dye bath. This shifts yellows to greens and interacts with tannins. Enameled cast iron that has chips exposing the metal works well as a source of iron. Unlined copper, brass, or tin all contribute metal ions when used as dye pots. Aluminum pots can add aluminum salts but can also react with acids or bases used as modifiers. These can eat holes in thin pots, leaking dye everywhere. If a non-reactive pot is unavailable, a large glass canning jar can be filled with dye and fiber and placed inside a kettle of water to heat. Make sure the glass is heat-stable.

Due to the ceramic liner, crock pots work well as both a pot and a heat source. Other heat sources include stoves and hot plates. For outdoor work, camp stoves or even a fire pit work well.

Stirring is essential when dyeing to get even coverage with the dye. Spoons, tongs, and even a stick all work equally well. Make sure to label the equipment for dye use only clearly. Because iron can absorb into wooden utensils and leach into a later dye pot, it is useful to label one tool as the iron tool, preventing cross-contamination.

Fiber Types

Different types of fibers are dyed differently. A silk scarf will take up color differently than a cotton yarn. Wool takes dyes differently than linen does. Even within similar types, loose fiber takes a dye differently than a yarn or a woven cloth. Different fibers require different preparations before actually dyeing the fibers. This does not mean that items containing two different types of fibers cannot be dyed with natural dyes. On the contrary, mixed fibers often give a more subtle or even heathery color. Just be aware of the fiber type or types in the dyed item. One caveat: synthetic fibers are most commonly made of a petroleum base and take natural dyes poorly. A small amount in a blended yarn is usually not a problem, but typically, the more synthetic, the lighter the color.

Animal fibers include wool, silk, fur, feathers, and leather. Cat and dog fur, camel or goat hairs and even human hair are animal fibers. These fibers are proteins. A protein molecule has a slight electrical charge to it. This is why silk and wool can build up static electricity. The charge allows the fibers to readily absorb the most natural dyes. Skin and nails also count as animal fibers, hence the importance of wearing gloves while working with dyes. Plant dyes can stain them fairly easily. Bone and shell buttons also contain proteins and can be dyed, although they usually do not stain as deeply and take longer to take up the dye due to their high mineral content.

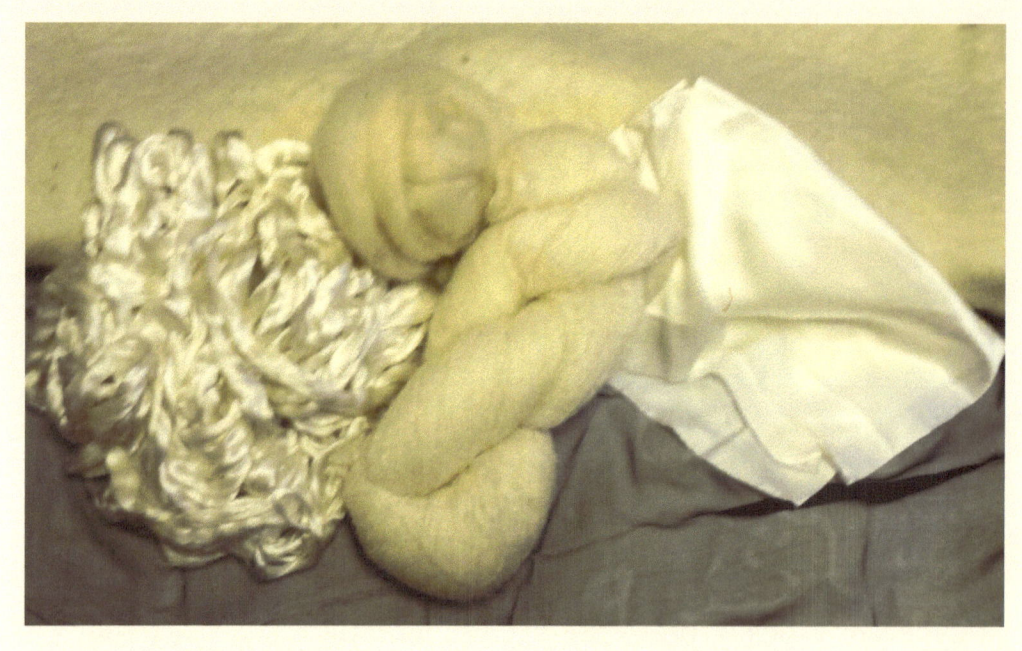

Animal fibers must first be washed to remove oils and dirt before being prepared for dyeing. Most yarns and other preprocessed fiber require just a single washing. Wool straight from the sheep usually requires two or more washings. Treat the fiber gently; wool can felt with abrupt temperature changes or too vigorous agitation. A mild dish soap or a cleanser specifically designed for fiber is recommended. It is gentlest to add the soap to cool water, add the fiber, and then slowly heat it. Protein fibers do not take abrupt changes in temperature without damage. Once the water has warmed to roughly bathwater temperature, slowly move the fibers to ensure all parts are exposed to the soapy solution. If the fibers are visibly dirty or feel oily, allow them to soak in the soap and water overnight. Rinse the fibers in warm water, again being careful not to agitate the fibers. Check how clean the rinse water is to determine if it needs additional cleaning. Oils and dirt can prevent dye penetration, so a second or even a third washing doesn't hurt. Once the fibers are clean, they can be dried or moved straight to the dye process.

Plant fibers are usually composed of cellulose. Linen, cotton, hemp, and bamboo are examples of cellulose fibers. Plant fibers are primarily made of complex carbohydrates. Carbohydrates do not usually carry a charge and do not pick up the dyes as strongly or may pick up different dye components than protein fibers. Wood and basket reed are also plant materials and can be dyed the same as cotton or linen. Plant fibers are not affected as strongly by temperature changes, nor do they felt, although unprocessed fiber can still tangle. While plant fibers do not usually contain oils, there can still be gums and lignin. Simmer plant fibers for an hour or more in a solution of water, soap, and washing soda, also known as soda ash or sodium carbonate. Rinse the fiber in warm water. If the rinse water looks discolored, repeat the washing process. Again, once clean, the fiber can be dried for later dyeing or used immediately.

Mordents & Modifiers

Natural dyes are referred to as being fast or being fugitive. Fast dyes keep their color on the fiber under normal use and light exposure. It will eventually fade over time, but not excessively. An example most people are familiar with is indigo. It usually takes years of wear and washing to fade. The plants in this book produce fast dyes.

One of the most frustrating experiences for a new dyer is to get a beautiful color, then have it wash out quickly or fade to another color. This is referred to as being fugitive. Quite literally, the color runs away. Many beginning dyers experiment with beet juice. It seems like a beautiful dye because it stains hands and fabric a bright pink. However, beet juice is a fugitive dye. In the sample below, the strand on top is fresh from a beet juice dye bath. The lower strand is the same yarn after being washed three times with laundry detergent. The original pink has faded to a grayish yellow.

Mordants are used to fix the dye to the fibers and keep the color. They can also adjust the color produced. Dyes that need mordants are referred to as being adjective dyes. Substantive dyes do not require mordants. Fibers can be treated before dyeing (pre-mordanting), or the mordant can be added to the dyebath (all-in-one dyebath). Some dyers have a collection of dye pots made of aluminum, iron, or copper, which can be used to dye, modify, and mordant the fibers at the same time.

Alum is the classic mordant for protein-based fibers. Alum is an aluminum salt and comes in several forms. A weak form of alum is used in pickling and can be found in the spice racks of most groceries. Aluminum sulfate, a stronger form of alum, can be found in garden centers. It is used to acidify the soil for blueberries and cranberries. If you use gardening aluminum sulfate, ensure no other minerals or fertilizers are added. These could further alter the color in unexpected ways. Most dye suppliers sell a purified form of aluminum sulfate. Some dyers use aluminum pots, although the amount of alum that leaches into the dye bath from the pot is minimal and difficult to control. Alum can be used alone or in combination with cream of tartar. Cream of tartar is a form of tartaric acid, an organic acid produced by grapes and several other fruits. It is often used in cooking and can be found in the spice racks at the grocery.

One standard method is to add a teaspoon of cream of tartar and two teaspoons of alum to a gallon of warm water and stir to dissolve. The fiber is then added and simmered for an hour. In the cold-soak method, the fiber is left overnight in the solution. No heat is used. Mordanted fibers can be used immediately or allowed to dry for later dyeing.

Alum alone is not adequate on plant fibers. The traditional method to mordant plant fiber is to simmer the washed fiber in a tannin solution for an hour or more before treating it with alum. Oak bark, oak or sumac leaves, or oak galls are simmered in water and then allowed to cool in the pot overnight. A functional but imprecise ratio of a handful of leaves to a gallon of water produces good results. It should resemble black tea. The solution is strained, the fiber to be dyed added, and the pot brought to a gentle simmer. Shut off the heat and allow it to cool. The fibers will pick up a beige-to-brown color. A teaspoon of alum can be added to the tannin bath to expand the color range and improve fastness.

Modifiers are added to shift the colors of the fibers. They can be added to the dye pot, used to pretreat fiber before dyeing, or used as a dip after dyeing. Using modifiers and mordants can dramatically expand the range of colors produced from a small number of dyes. Modifiers include acids, bases, and metals.

Using acids or bases to adjust the pH of the dye bath or treating the fibers after dyeing is a common method of modifying a dye. Test the pH of water with pH test strips available at most dye suppliers, hydroponics suppliers, garden centers, and aquarium suppliers. The pH scale runs from 0 to 14, with 7 being neutral. Any pH below 7 is considered acidic; those above 7 are considered basic or alkaline. Most municipal water supplies are adjusted to near neutral. Distilled water is also in the neutral zone. The pH of rainwater is around 5.6, putting it in the acidic range. Well water varies dramatically. The closer to pH 0, the stronger the acid is. Vinegar and citric acid are common acids added to lower the pH. Many old dye books recommend using bog water for dyeing. The water in a bog is acidic, often around pH 4, and rich in tannins, giving it a brown undertone and making it useful for pretreating plant fibers. Other options include soured beer, wine, or citrus juices. Anything above pH 7 is considered basic or alkaline. The closer to pH 14, the stronger a base is. Washing soda, wood ash, and household ammonia are common bases used to raise pH. Before the availability of modern chemicals, stale urine or wood ashes were used to raise the pH. Both very strong acids and very strong bases can be hard on fibers and should be used with care. The effects of altering the pH vary depending on the specific dye plant. For example, buckthorn berries produce a fast green under basic conditions and a fugitive pink under acidic conditions.

Iron is one of the easiest metals to use. It is both a modifier and a mordant. Powdered iron, in the form of ferrous sulfate, can be purchased from dye suppliers. Being concentrated and a powder, a mask should be worn when handling it. A DIY iron solution can be made by covering rusty metal scraps with a solution of 50% water and 50% vinegar. Allow this to sit for several days to weeks. The liquid will become rusty-colored. This can be added to the dye bath or used as a pre-mordant. If adding it to the dye bath, dilute it with water and stir constantly when adding. Otherwise, the fiber can become splotchy. The easiest way to use iron is to dye in a cast iron pot. Iron tends to shift yellow dyes toward greens, pinks toward purple, and anything rich in tannins toward grays.

Various forms of copper have been used as a mordant and as a modifier. While copper salts can be purchased, a DIY copper solution is easy to make. Cover scraps of copper wire or pipe with a solution of 50% water and 50% vinegar. Do not use modern pennies. They have only a tiny bit of copper over other metals. Allow the solution to stand and be covered for several weeks. A pinch of sea salt tends to speed up the reaction. Over time, the solution will turn a beautiful blue. This can be poured off and added to either a dye bath or the alum mordanting solution. When used as a mordant for wool, the fiber turns blue-green. Copper brings up the blues and greens.

Other metals have also been used as modifiers, though these are more difficult to come by these days and require more precautions. Tin and titanium are fairly safe to use. They can sometimes be found at chemical or paint supply houses. Older dye books will mention both chrome and arsenic. While both of these give gorgeous colors, they are highly toxic and should not be used.

All mordants and modifiers should be stored out of reach of children and pets. They should be clearly labeled. Premordanted fibers should also be labeled.

Methods

There are multiple methods for getting color into the fiber once it has been scrubbed and mordanted. A dye bath, contact dyeing, and solar dyeing are three common methods, with a dye bath being the most common.

The first step in a dye bath is to remove the dye from the source material. There are various methods that work with different materials. Water is the common liquid used, but experiment. Some pigments are soluble in alcohol rather than water. If using alcohol, be careful to avoid open flames when heating the dye bath.

Soft materials can be chopped or torn into small bits before processing. This increases the surface area and helps the colors leach out. This works well with leaves and flower parts. Harder materials like wood or bark can be grated, chipped, or shaved. Barks also benefit from soaking before processing. Most barks contain large amounts of tannins, which are released when boiled. Tannins add a brown color to the dyes. If you don't want the tannins, keep the temperatures lower when extracting the dyes.

Soaking dyestuffs in hot water is one of the oldest dye methods and the one most people are familiar with. The dye material is heated in water, allowed to steep, and the dye liquid is strained off for use. The fibers are then added to the bath, and they absorb the color. Some dyers prefer to leave the plant material in with the fiber but contain it in a bag. Whichever method is used, the bath is heated with the fiber and held at a simmer for an hour or more, and the fiber is allowed to cool in the bath to produce deeper, more permanent results.

Heat helps release the pigments and fix them to the fibers. Dyes can be heated on a stove or fire. Don't allow the dye bath to get too low. The fibers need to keep moving for even dyeing. Adding additional water will not affect the dyeing process. When working with wool, avoid abrupt temperature changes, agitation, and hard boiling. This can felt the fibers. Typically, you want a gentle simmer.

Another method is to use solar dye. The dye and fiber are placed in a jar or plastic bag and left in the sun for several days. Solar dyeing takes longer but minimizes the chance of felting and requires little tending. It works especially well with very delicate fibers. Just set it up and walk away.

Fermentation by microorganisms can produce dyes that are not present in the original plant material. The microbes digest components within the source material and release the breakdown products. The fermentation process also alters the pH and the oxygen levels in the bath. The fermentation of indigo is one of the classic examples. Barks and fruits also react well to fermentation methods. Fair warning about fermentation—it takes a while, and it is often quite aromatic. Do not seal fermentation containers. They can fill with gas and explode, creating a mess. Fermented baths can be used with either heat or with solar dyeing.

Contact dyeing is one of the easiest methods. The dye material is laid directly on the wetted fiber, and the dye seeps into the fiber. Heat may be applied. This method lends itself especially well to solar dyeing. The results are often uneven, with color more concentrated in some areas and leaving others with no color. The technique produces some interesting patterns on cloth and gives a tweed effect to yarns. Eco-dyeing is a modern version of contact dyeing.

Over-dyeing is a process where fiber is dyed one color and then dyed again with a second color. Using this technique can dramatically expand the range of colors from a relatively few basic dyes. Not all over-dyeing produces the expected results.

Dye books and blogs sometimes use the term exhaust. There is usually some pigment still in the water after a dye bath. Introducing more fiber into the "exhausted" bath will produce lighter colors. This is good for producing a variety of shades in a single color or for combining dyes. The first exhaust bath is after the initial dyeing. A second exhaust uses what is left after the first exhaust. Some dyes can give three or four exhaust baths. In the photo below, buckthorn bark was soaked in ammonia and water for several days before filtering and heating in a dye bath. The sample on the left is from the initial dye bath. The middle sample is the yarn from the first exhaust bath. The sample on the right is from the second exhaust bath.

HOW To USE THIS BOOK

Natural dyeing is an art form; every artist has their own approach. This book is designed to be a guide, not a rule book. Feel free to experiment, always keeping safety in mind.

The samples shown were all produced using a 90% merino and 10% nylon sock yarn. The dyes were all produced using a heated dye bath unless otherwise stated. Equal weights of yarn and fresh plant material were used. A single pot of each plant was prepared and filtered. It was then split for the different treatments. Alum and modifiers were added to the pots in an all-in-one process. For each plant listed, there is a dye card with multiple samples. The samples on the card are in the following order:

The acid used was household vinegar. The base used was household ammonia. The iron was the DIY rusty water.

NOTES

INTRODUCING THE INVASIVE PLANTS

AMUR MAPLE

(Acer ginnala)

Amur maple was imported from Asia as a landscape tree due to its height and brilliant fall color. It rarely exceeds a height of 20 feet (6 meters), making it well-suited under power lines and in smaller yards. It produces beautiful scarlet and orange foliage come fall. The leaves are opposite, three-lobed with doubly serrated edges, and smaller than other members of the maple family. The rapid and dense growth creates windbreaks and shelters wildlife. The tree bark is light grayish brown and quite smooth. Amur maple produces clusters of pale yellow flowers in the spring and, like other members of the maple family, produces huge numbers of helicopter-like seedpods, called samaras, in the fall.

The tree is very adaptable, growing in both sun and shade. It tolerates both wet and dry conditions. The large number of samara produced sprout easily, and the tree grows more rapidly than other maples. Squirrels and chipmunks gather the samara, helping to distribute the seeds. Amur maples resprout from cut stumps, increasing their survivability. The leaves have a bitter flavor, and few creatures graze on them.

Preventing Amur maples from spreading requires raking up and destroying the samara and removing young plants. The root system is shallow, making it fairly easy to pull seedlings.

Both the bark and the leaves of Amur maples produce dyes. For tan or gray, peel bark from the larger branches. Place the fresh bark in a dye pot and cover it with water. Bring the bark to a low boil and hold it there for 30 minutes or more. Longer produces deeper colors. Strain and return the dye liquid to the pot. Add your fiber and simmer gently for an hour. The addition of iron turns the yarn into a rich gray.

Amur maple leaves also produce a variety of shades depending on the mordants and modifiers used. Gather the fresh leaves and simmer for 30 minutes. Strain and return the dye to the pot. Add the fiber and any modifier. Simmer for another 30 minutes and allow to cool overnight in the pot. Alum and acid produce light yellow, with bases bringing out a bright gold. The addition of iron shifts the color to a greenish gold.

Dye Colors from Bark — *Dye Colors from Leaves*

- No mordant
- Alum, pH 7
- Alum, pH 4
- Alum, pH 10
- Alum & iron

BIG-LEAF LUPINE

(Lupinus polyphyllus)

Lupines are beautiful wildflowers. This member of the legume family, these 3-foot (1 meter) tall perennials produce a central flower spike with a terminal cluster of blossoms ranging in color from white to pink to the more common deep purple/blue. The plant gets its name from the large, palmately compound leaves with up to a dozen or more leaflets. Big-leaf lupine is native to the Pacific Northwest, primarily British Columbia and Washington state. However, gardeners spread the plants eastward and to other countries where they have displaced native lupines. In early summer, roadsides are frequently covered with the purple spikes of the lovely but invasive plants.

As legume family members, lupines can fix their own nitrogen, giving them an advantage over other plants in areas with poor or disturbed soil. Each flower can become a fuzzy seed pod with up to a dozen small, hard seeds inside. When ripe, the pods burst open, scattering seed. This can lead to large clumps that exclude other plants. The beauty of the plant has led people to plant it in gardens, from which it readily escapes, and to scatter the seeds along roadways. The masses of blooms are gorgeous but still damaging to non-native ecosystems.

One of the easiest ways to control the spread of this lupine is not to plant it in the garden. Look for a native lupine instead. If big-leaf lupines are already growing in the area, cut the flower heads or mow the area before the seeds are set. The plants do not tolerate repeated mowing during the growing season.

For dye purposes, the dark purple flowers produce the best color. Use a ratio of 2 times the weight of flowers to fiber. The other flowers produce very, very pale dyes, even with 3 or 4 times the weight of flowers to fiber. Pull the flowers off the central stem, crush them, and place them in the pot. Cover with water and simmer the flowers for 30 minutes. Strain the dye liquid and add the fiber to it. Simmer for another 30 minutes, add modifiers if desired, and allow the fiber to cool in the pot. The fibers come out a pale seafoam green. Contact dyeing with the leaves produces a chartreuse print.

BIRDSFOOT TREFOIL

(Lotus corniculatus)

The bright yellow, pea-type flowers of birdsfoot trefoil brighten the disturbed soils along roadsides and parking lots. The flowers appear in flat clusters of up to a dozen atop low-growing stems. The compound flowers resemble clover with three leaflets and have two whisker-like stipules, and the leaf attaches to the stem. The stems can reach up to 2 feet (75cm) under ideal conditions, though they usually grow shorter, spreading along the ground. The seedpods resemble the tiny toes of a bird, hence the name. Each pod can contain two dozen seeds.

Birdsfoot trefoil was introduced from Europe as livestock feed, particularly forage mixtures. It readily takes over prairie areas and meadows. Due to its long taproot, the plant has also been used for erosion control along highways. Like other legume family members, it can fix nitrogen, giving it a nutrient advantage over other plants. This allows it to produce large mats of vegetation, crowding out and overshadowing other plants. The plant can regrow from the taproot, allowing it to survive prairie fires and trampling by animals.

Frequent mowing over several seasons is the best way to control birdsfoot trefoil without using chemical herbicides.

When used as a dye, the whole plant is pulled, chopped, and added to the dye pot. Cover with water and bring to a simmer for roughly an hour. Strain out the plant material before adding the yarn. If using a modifier, add it at this point, then simmer for an hour. Allow the fiber to cool in the pot overnight. Birdsfoot trefoil gives shades of beige to a warm light gray.

BRADFORD PEAR

(Pyrus calleryana)

Bradford pears are an ornamental pear tree grown for the profusion of white flower clusters produced in the spring. Bees feed heavily on the 5-petaled flowers. The fruit is a quarter-sized, hard pear, too small for harvesting, and the flavor is slightly bitter. The leaves are leathery, with a wavy edge, and come off the branches in an alternate arrangement. The bark of smaller branches is smooth, but larger branches and the main truck are furrowed. The branches often have stiff, wicked thorns. The tree was introduced from its native Asia into the landscape trade.

The small fruits are eaten by birds, squirrels, and deer, who spread the seeds. Seedlings can grow in a variety of soil conditions. The thorns protect the plant from heavy grazing, though deer eat individual leaves. The trees grow very rapidly and can create an almost impenetrable wall when growing in clusters. The dense foliage shades out other plants. The trees are prone to cracking, and large branches easily break off and fall.

Most landscapers no longer plant the Bradford pear, which is still found in some nursery catalogs. Seedlings can be pulled or mowed when small to control the species. Larger trees can be cut but will often resprout from the stump, so it may take diligence to remove them. Large trees may also be girdled.

Both the leaves and the bark of this pear produce dyes. Harvest fresh leaves from midsummer into early fall for the best color. Cover the leaves with water and bring to a simmer. The leathery nature of the leave requires a little longer to break down, so simmer for about an hour. Strain out the leaves and add the fiber and any modifier. Simmer this for an hour and allow the fiber to cool in the pot overnight. Under neutral or acidic conditions, the color is a shade of beige to tan. Basic conditions bring out yellow golds. The addition of iron produces green.

The bark produces a completely different color. Use a sharp knife to gather bark from the main trunk or from larger branches. Cut down to the level of the wood. Avoid small twigs. They produce poor color. Simmer the bark for an hour and allow it to soak overnight. Do not boil, or the brown tannins are extracted. Strain out the bark and add the fiber and any modifier. Simmer for 30 minutes or more to obtain the deeper colors. The bark produces shades of pink. Acids bring out a more salmon color, while adding iron shifts it to purplish.

Dye Colors from Bark — *Dye Colors from Leaves*

- No mordant
- Alum, pH 7
- Alum, pH 4
- Alum, pH 10
- Alum & iron

BUCKTHORN

Common (Rhamnus cathartica)

Glossy (Frangula alnus)

Both common and glossy buckthorn are highly aggressive invasive species. Both were brought from Europe to create thick, thorny hedgerows. Both species grow to about 20 feet (6m), have dark brown bark with gray spots, produce black to dark purple berries, and have small, alternate, oval leaves. The common buckthorn leaves are slightly toothed, and the leaf tip is pointed. Glossy buckthorn leaves are smooth-edged and lack a point. The leaves of both species stay green into early winter before dropping. The berries have been used medicinally as a strong laxative. Woodcarvers also prize the wood for its beautiful color and easy workability.

Buckthorn grows rapidly and aggressively. Few animals or insects eat the leaves. However, berries are common food for birds. These have a laxative effect on the birds, spreading the seeds. Seeds stay viable in the soil for two years or more, and germination rates are high. This, combined with the tree's ability to sprout from its network of roots and stumps, creates thickets that crowd out native trees and shrubs and shade out undergrowth. Thickets can be dense enough to block access to water, further degrading wildlife habitat.

Buckthorn removal is difficult. The first priority is the removal of trees mature enough to produce berries. This prevents new seeds from being spread. When cut, the tree can resprout from the stump. Cut trees either need to be completely covered so new growth does not have access to light, or the stump needs treatment with an herbicide. It may require several years to kill a tree. The fibrous root network makes it difficult to pull any seedlings but the smallest. Communities often hold buckthorn pulls, a community event to clear buckthorn from a specific area.

For all the problems it creates, buckthorn is one of the most versatile dye plants. The bark provides the broadest range of dyes, so you can help control the invasive species while getting good dye at the same time. The bark separates most easily in the spring and early summer, but buckthorn bark can be gathered any time of year. Use a sharp knife to strip the bark from the tree. Beware the thorns. Freshly peeled bark appears yellow to orange. It rapidly oxidizes and turns nearly black. This does not alter the dye produced. It can be used immediately or dried for later use. Buckthorn bark also works extremely well for contact dyeing, giving gold to red-brown.

How the bark is treated determines the colors. Whatever method you choose, strain the bark out before adding your fiber. The bark shreds are difficult to remove if left in the pot with the fiber.

BUCKTHORN *(Continued)*

To produce shades of light gold to orangey brown, pour boiling water over the bark and allow it to soak for an hour or so before straining and adding the fiber.

Boiling the bark for 30 minutes to an hour before straining and adding the fiber produces deep golden browns.

Soaking the bark in a solution of half household ammonia and half water for several days, straining, then gently heating the fiber in the dye bath produces reddish browns to dark browns. If inhaled, ammonia is potent and toxic, so use a respirator or work outside.

Fresh buckthorn leaves produce yellows to golds. Buckthorn holds its leaves well into the winter. One easy way to identify a stand of buckthorn is to look for the still-green leaves in December, long after all the other trees have dropped their leaves. This is one of the few yellows that does not shift green with the addition of an iron modifier.

Fresh, ripe buckthorn berries, gathered in the fall and early winter, produce beautiful greens. Buckthorn berries were the original source for the sap green used by painters. The berries are sticky when picked, so disposable gloves are recommended. Remember their laxative properties. Again, beware of the thorns on the branches. Cover the berries with water

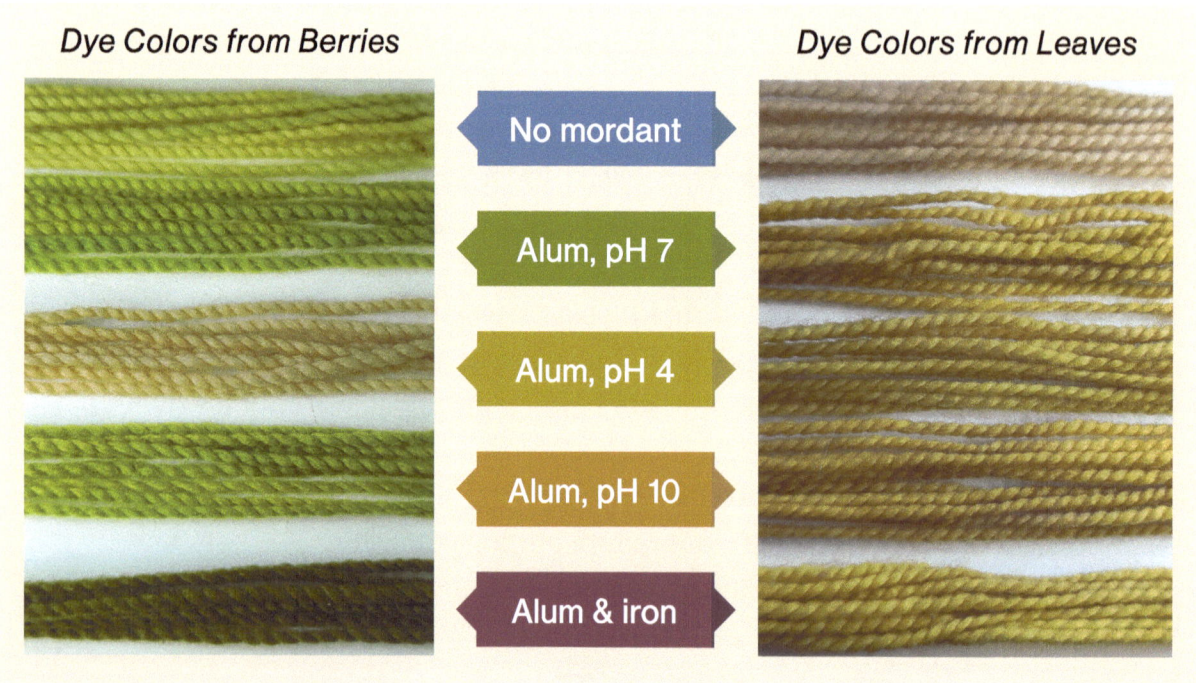

and simmer for an hour or more. If the berries are still whole, continue simmering until they begin to break apart. Remove from the heat and allow to cool before straining. Return the strained dye to the pot and add fiber and any modifier. Simmer for an hour and allow to cool in the pot. The addition of a base creates a brighter green. The addition of iron produces dark greens. Acid produces a pink, which is neither light nor washing fast. This sample has been kept in the dark to retain its color.

NOTES

CREEPING BELLFLOWER

(Campanula rapunculoides)

With its spike of blue, 1-inch (2.54 cm) bell-shaped flowers, the creeping bellflower makes a lovely addition to the garden, explaining why it was introduced from its native Eurasia. Unfortunately, it refuses to stay in the garden. The 3-foot (1m) flower spikes bloom from the lowest to the top. The plant can have ripe seed pods, blooming flowers, and new buds all at the same time. That spike rises from a circle of 3-inch (7.5 cm) leaves with serrated edges. Smaller leaves are more elongated and are spaced along the lower 1/3 of the stem, merging into the flowers. The roots are spreading and can form a long taproot.

Creeping bellflower produces thousands of seeds per plant. It can also sprout from segments of the taproot that break off. This combination allows the plant to spread rapidly, creating dense growth and crowding out native plants. The plant is adapted to almost any soil type and growing conditions, from cracks in sidewalks to meadows and ditches.

The ability of creeping bellflower to grow from small fragments makes it difficult to control. The taproot can extend a foot (30 cm) deep. Pulling leaves root fragments. Digging the plants out is time-consuming, and fragments are often produced in the process. Removing the flowering stalk before seeds develop can slow the spread. Covering areas with landscape paper or cardboard for a year can prevent seeds from sprouting. Herbicides are largely ineffective as the plant has developed a resistance to them.

The entire above-ground parts of the plant can be used as a dye source. While the primary color obtained from a vat dye is beige to light tan, the addition of iron produces a lovely gray-green. Doubling or even tripling the ratio of plant material to fiber produces darker shades. The blue flowers do not produce a dye in a vat dye; they will print blue in contact dyeing.

No mordant

Alum, pH 7

Alum, pH 4

Alum, pH 10

Alum & iron

CREEPING CHARLIE

(Glechoma hederacea)

Creeping Charlie goes by various names, including gill over the ground and ground ivy. Its square stems and strong aroma identify it as a member of the mint family. It was introduced to North America by early settlers for its use as a medicine and food. It is evergreen and one of the earliest plants to be foraged in the spring. The leaves are small, shiny, and round with scalloped edges. They appear as opposite pairs at the stem nodes. The stems both spread along the ground and branch upward, reaching a height of up to a foot (30cm). In the spring, the plant produces small, purple-blue, tube-shaped flowers that bees visit.

Creeping Charlie primarily spreads vegetative growth. Each node that touches the ground develops roots. The fragile stems easily break, allowing the plant to spread. The plant grows rapidly and can spread over lawns, gardens, and undeveloped areas. It creates a heavy mat of tangled growth and can crowd out native plants.

The best method to control Creeping Charlie is to physically remove it. Pull the plants, loosening the soil around the nodes to prevent breakage. In lawns, mowing can control the growth. Do not add all the material to a compost pile because the fragments will root.

Creeping Charlie works well as a vat dye. Pull the whole plant and use it fresh. Cover the plants with water and simmer for 30 minutes. Strain the liquid and add the fiber and any modifiers. Simmer for another 30 minutes and allow the fiber to cool in the pot. Creeping Charlie produces a tan dye that will shift to agray-greenn with the addition of iron.

CURLY DOCK

(Rumex crispus)

Curly dock is a native of Africa and Eurasia, although it is now found almost globally. Perhaps the most distinct characteristic of curly dock is the 3-foot (1-meter) branched seed stalk covered in deep russet brown seed that ripens late summer into fall and remains on the stalk for much of the winter, providing food for birds. Each seed is surrounded by a papery, heart-shaped structure. The plant is a perennial with a long taproot. The leaves form a dense rosette at the base, with the leaves radiating outward and upward. They are long and somewhat narrow with a strong midrib and distinctly wavy, or curl, edge from which the plant gets its common name.

The large number of seeds curly dock produces spread easily. The plant is highly adaptable, growing from tropical areas to the cold north, and it tolerates a broad range of soil types. It outcompetes native species.

Curly dock's long taproot makes it difficult to pull. Plants cut or mowed near the surface regrow from the taproot. Removing the seed stalk slows the spread, so mowing can be used to control it.

The brown seeds dye wool shades of rosy tan. Pull the ripe seeds from the stalk and cover them with water. Simmer for 30 minutes, then strain. Make sure to get all the seeds out. The papery covering sticks to the fiber. Add the fiber and any modifier and simmer for an hour. Allow the fiber to cool in the pot. If doing a contact dye, sprinkle the seeds onto the fabric. They create fun little pops of color.

CUTLEAF TEASEL

(Dipsacus laciniatus)

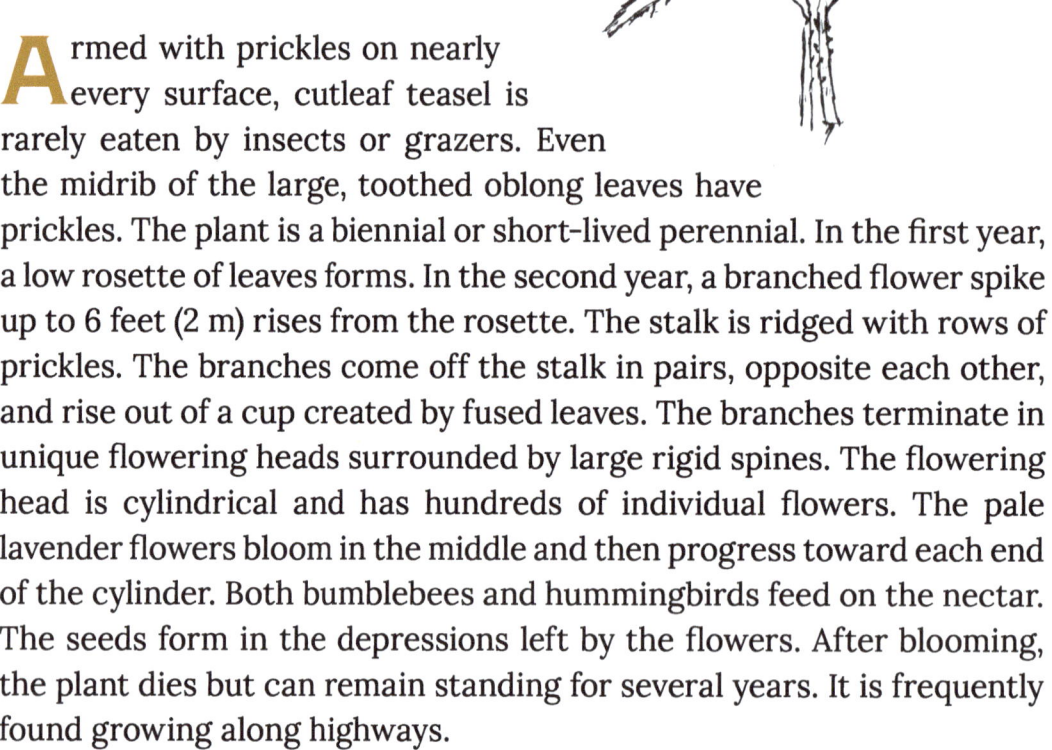

Armed with prickles on nearly every surface, cutleaf teasel is rarely eaten by insects or grazers. Even the midrib of the large, toothed oblong leaves have prickles. The plant is a biennial or short-lived perennial. In the first year, a low rosette of leaves forms. In the second year, a branched flower spike up to 6 feet (2 m) rises from the rosette. The stalk is ridged with rows of prickles. The branches come off the stalk in pairs, opposite each other, and rise out of a cup created by fused leaves. The branches terminate in unique flowering heads surrounded by large rigid spines. The flowering head is cylindrical and has hundreds of individual flowers. The pale lavender flowers bloom in the middle and then progress toward each end of the cylinder. Both bumblebees and hummingbirds feed on the nectar. The seeds form in the depressions left by the flowers. After blooming, the plant dies but can remain standing for several years. It is frequently found growing along highways.

Teasel was brought from Europe both as a garden plant and for using the heads to manufacture fabric. Split heads were used for carding wool, and whole heads were used to raise the knap on fabric. The plant is still used in wreaths and flower arrangements.

Teasel spreads its seed via bird, and anything that bends the stalks allows the seed to fall out. If the heads have not been deseeded, they continue to shed seeds when used in wreaths and flower arrangements, producing new plants. The plants can create dense stands that crowd out native vegetation and deprive grazers of food.

Mowing is limited in its effectiveness at controlling teasel. In response to being mowed, the plant grows a much shorter stalk. In some cases, the heads will appear at ground level. Teasel can be dug out. Removing the seed head immediately after blooming can also control the spread since the plant dies after blooming.

Teasel leaves produce yellow and yellow-green on wool. Harvest fresh leaves, remembering to wear heavy leather gloves. The prickles are vicious and will penetrate clothing and lighter-weight gloves. Cover the leaves with water and simmer for up to an hour before straining. Add the fiber and any modifiers, simmer for another hour, then allow to cool in the pot. Teasel is not good for contact dyeing because the prickles catch on the fabric and can damage it.

JAPANESE KNoTWEED

(Reynoutria japonica)

Japanese knotweed is also referred to as Japanese bamboo, but it is not a true bamboo. True bamboo is a grass, while Japanese knotweed is a broadleaf plant. The hollow, reddish-speckled stems appear jointed, like true bamboo, but it is semi-woody, and the fragile stems break easily. The stems can reach up to 10 feet (3 m) and have an alternate branching pattern. The leaves are large, up to 6 inches (15 cm) long and 4 inches (10 cm) wide, and slightly heart-shaped, tapering to a point at the tip. The leaves create a dense canopy. Long clusters of tiny white flowers arise in late summer from the leaf nodes. The plant is native to Asia and was introduced via the landscape trade due to its dense growth, beautiful white flowers, and unique stems. It thrives on neglect, making it ideal for low-maintenance landscapes, so it was widely planted.

Unfortunately, Japanese knotweed is now considered one of the most aggressive invasive species in the world. Tradition control methods, such as cutting, burning, and herbicides, often kill vegetative growth, but it can grow back from its extensive and far-reaching rhizome network. Rhizomes can spread underground across roads, through barriers, and even through cracks in concrete. In addition, it can reproduce via seed and vegetatively from plant parts. Plants that are removed should not be composed because they can sprout. The dense growth and layers of overlapping leaves shade out the undergrowth and outcompete native species. The rhizomes have the potential to damage pipes and even foundations.

Removal of Japanese knotweed is difficult and often best left to professionals. Digging is ineffective due to the extensive rhizome network and the plant's ability to regenerate from small bits. Removing all the above-ground growth is used in some places, but it requires weekly attention to remove all the sprouts. Over-the-counter herbicides are also not very effective.

    Harvest the leaves and chop down the stems (dry and burn them) to obtain dyes. Bring the leaves to a simmer for 30 minutes to an hour, then strain the dye liquid. Dry the leaves and burn them. Add the fiber and any modifiers. Simmer for an hour and allow to cool in the pot overnight. Shades range from gold to a greenish brown. The leaves and smaller stems print well in contact dyeing, creating gold or reddish-brown prints.

NOTES

MULLEIN

(Verbascum thapsus)

With its soft, fuzzy leaves and tall flower stalk, common mullein is children's favorite to play with. The plant is native to Eurasia and appeared in North America during colonial times. It has been used for millennia as a medicine and a dye. As with many plants with long histories of use, mullein has a variety of other common names, including flannel leaf, witch's taper, lambs ears, and rouge leaf. The tall seed heads have been dipped in tallow to produce torches. The leaves have been used padded fabric, and rubbing them on the skin increases circulation and brings a blush to the skin.

It is a biennial, with first-year plants producing a low rosette of large leaves, up to a foot long (30 cm) and nearly as wide. The leaves are covered with soft hairs that give them a velvet-like feel and a pale green or silvered appearance. In the second year, a tall stalk rises from the center of the rosette, reaching 6 feet (2 m) or more in height. The stalk is usually unbranched and has smaller leaves on the lower third. The stalk is covered with tightly packed, 1-inch (2.54 cm) bright yellow flowers with five petals. The flowers give way to a round brown seed pod filled with tiny seeds. After blooming, the plant dies. The seed stalks remain standing through the winter.

Mullein produces large quantities of seeds that can remain viable in the soil for decades. The seeds need light to germinate, so anything that disturbs the soil can bring them to the surface where they sprout. It thrives in dry and disturbed soils, making it one of the early plants to emerge and colonize abandoned fields, roadside ditches, and burn scars. The large rosette of leaves shades out other emerging species. While wildlife will graze on mullein leaves, domestic livestock avoid it. Large numbers of seeds can be toxic to fish.

For smaller infestations, the plants can be removed by digging out the long taproot. Removal of the seed head before the pods ripen can control the spread. Mullein is difficult to eradicate once established due to the long life of the seeds.

Historically, mullein flowers were used as a yellow dye source for hair and fiber. They are prepared for vat dyes by simmering with water. The addition of the leaves to the dye bath produces slightly greener yellows. The flowers produce bright yellow prints when contact dyeing. However, the velvety hairs on the leaves prevent good contact and produce poor prints.

NORWAY MAPLE

(Acer platanoides)

Norway maple was introduced from Europe as a shade tree along city streets. The tree is highly tolerant of air pollution produced by city traffic. Several varieties produce reddish-purple pigments during the growing season, making the tree valuable as a pop of color in the landscape. The leaves have the traditional maple look, palmate with five lobes and deep teeth widely spaced along the margins. They come off the branches in pairs, opposite each other. The sap is milky white and bitter. The bark is smooth and grayish in young trees and becomes ridged and more brown in older trees. When left unpruned, a mature tree can reach 60 feet (18 m). Small yellow-green flowers appear in the spring, followed by samara, the helicopter-like seeds.

Norway maples are competitive over native maples, such as sugar maples. They grow more rapidly and tolerate more adverse conditions than native maples. The dense canopy can shade out wildflowers and seedlings of other species, reducing diversity in the plant community. In addition, the roots are very shallow, potentially depriving other plants of nutrients in wild areas and damaging infrastructure in urban environments. The milky sap's bitter flavor discourages nibbling by insects and herbivores, especially in seedlings.

It is best to avoid planting Norway maples. In areas where they are already established, the larger trees can be removed and the stumps treated to prevent sucker formation and growth. Seedlings are fairly easy to pull due to the shallow root system.

The reddish purple-leaved varieties produce an interesting range of colors. In contact dyeing, they print purplish. Treating the fabric with vinegar before placing the leaves gives more of a pink print. When vat dyeing, keep the temperature lower and add more bathwater than a simmer to produce the best colors. The colors range from a pink that is not particularly lightfast under acidic conditions to a rich honey brown under basic conditions to a delicate purple-gray with the addition of iron.

Solar dyeing can produce a more stable pink. Put fiber pretreated with alum and whole leaves in a glass jar or clear plastic bag. Cover with equal parts water and vinegar. Seal the container or bag and place it in a sunny spot for up to a week. This long, slow, but cooler process seems to give a dye that is faster than vat dyeing.

ORANGE HAWKWEED

(Hieracium aurantiacum)

A European native, orange hawkweed can create beautiful displays in the early summer, carpeting lawns and roadsides. After the first mass showing, smaller numbers of scattered plants will continue to bloom until frost. The flowers resemble small dandelions, with small flower heads (3/4 inch or 2cm) and multiple rectangular petals radiating from the flower center. The petals are yellow-orange in the center and shade deep orange at the ends. In Britain, the plant is referred to as fox and cubs. The fox is the center head, and the cubs are the green flower buds surrounding it. The flowers mature into white tufts, similar to dandelions, which can be carried on the wind for dispersal. The tufts are slightly sticky and will also adhere to clothing and fur. A cluster of flowers is usually at the top of a foot-long (30cm) thin stem. The leaves are no more than 5 inches long (12cm), usually smaller and rounded, and form a ground-level rosette. The leaves and stems are covered with small hairs that secrete a sticky sap.

Orange hawkweed rapidly colonizes lawns, fields, and other open areas. The seeds can remain viable in the soil for several years. The plant appears to secrete chemicals that inhibit the growth of other plants, a process called allelopathy. Combined with its dense growth habit, it outcompetes many native species and creates monocultures.

Once established, orange hawkweed is difficult to remove. Mowing can reduce seed production, but because the plant is a perennial, it will grow back. In small infestations, the plants can be pulled.

The flower heads of orange hawkweed produce a variety of shades with vat dyeing resembling a sunrise. Pick the flowers and use them immediately. The flowers rapidly turn to fluff when picked. Create a dye vat by covering the flowers with water. Pull away the buds and only use the open flowers. Simmer them gently for 30 minutes and strain through a fine sieve or cloth. The petals tend to separate in the dye bath and stick to the fiber, if not all removed. Add the prepared fiber and any modifiers and simmer for another 30 minutes. Remove the fiber. Do not allow the fiber to cool in the dye bath; it shifts the color brownish. Alum alone produces a rosy pink. Acids shift their color to a yellow-orange. The addition of a base produces bright oranges. The flowers do not work well in contract dyes due to the sticky sap.

PURPLE LOOSESTRIFE

(Lythrum salicaria)

Purple loosestrife is a European native perennial introduced as a garden plant for its lush masses of bright magenta flowers and its ability to thrive in wet areas that many other flowers will not tolerate. The plant produces dozens of branches and can reach a light of 3 feet (1 m). The leaves change shape along these woody branches. Those at the base are nearly heart-shaped. Further up the branches, they become lance-shaped. In late summer to early fall, the upper portions of each branch produce flower spikes up to 15 inches (38cm) long, covered with magenta blossoms. Each flower is less than 3/4 inch (2 cm), has 4 to 7 petals, and has twice as many stamens. A single plant can produce well over a million seeds.

Despite the beauty of masses of blooming purple loosestrife, it is a highly damaging invasive. Its seed can be spread via flowing water or as a hitchhiker in pleasure craft and ship ballast. The plant grows aggressively, producing tangled walls of vegetation, crowding out native aquatic species used by animals and waterfowl for food and shelter. Once introduced into an aquatic environment, it takes over. Entire wetland areas become clogged with plants, and drainage ditches can become blocked with their dense root system.

Purple loosestrife responds well to biological controls using insects imported from its native habitat. Several beetle species only eat loosestrife, so they pose no threat to native plant communities. Carefully cleaning boats and other equipment that have been in areas prevents it from spreading to new areas.

When dyeing with purple loosestrife, the entire plant can be used. Pull it out, chop it up, and toss it in the pot. Cover it with water and simmer for an hour before straining. Add the fiber and simmer for an hour. After the fiber has picked up the dye, then add any modifiers. Acids and bases produce warm beige. The addition of iron produces a deep gray with a hint of purple.

QUEEN ANNE'S LACE

(Daucus carota)

With its lacy flower heads, Queen Anne's lace looks perfectly at home in a flower garden. It is the Eurasian wild ancestor of the modern carrot. Early settlers used Queen Anne's lace medicinally to treat digestive issues and its effects on the reproductive system. The first-year plant produces long, pale yellow to white taproots. The leaves are up to 8 inches (20 cm) and twice pinnately compound, with finely divided leaflets found in modern carrots. The leaves rise from the crown of the root. The entire plant smells like carrots, but the root is often bitter, and some people are sensitive to the sap and root. The second-year plant sends up a hollow, branched flower stalk. It can reach a height of 3 feet (1 m). The branches end in a flat-topped umbel—many small, four-petaled flowers atop short stems. The center flower of the umbel is dark, a purple-red color. After the flowers bloom, the umbel curls inward, creating almost a basket. The seeds are small, flattened ovals.

The plant invades disturbed areas, prairies, and roadsides, displacing native species. However, bees and butterflies feed on the flowers. Queen Anne's lace is sometimes included in wildflower seed mixes.

Removing the flowers prevents the formation of seeds and stops the spread of the plant.

Queen Anne's lace leaves produce yellow-green dyes when vat dyeing. Use three to four times the weight of plant material to fiber to get deeper shades. Cover the plant material with water and gently simmer to release the pigments. High heat can shift the color to brown. Strain the dye and add modifiers, if desired. The addition of iron produces the greenest shade. Simmer for another 30 minutes and allow to cool in the dye bath.

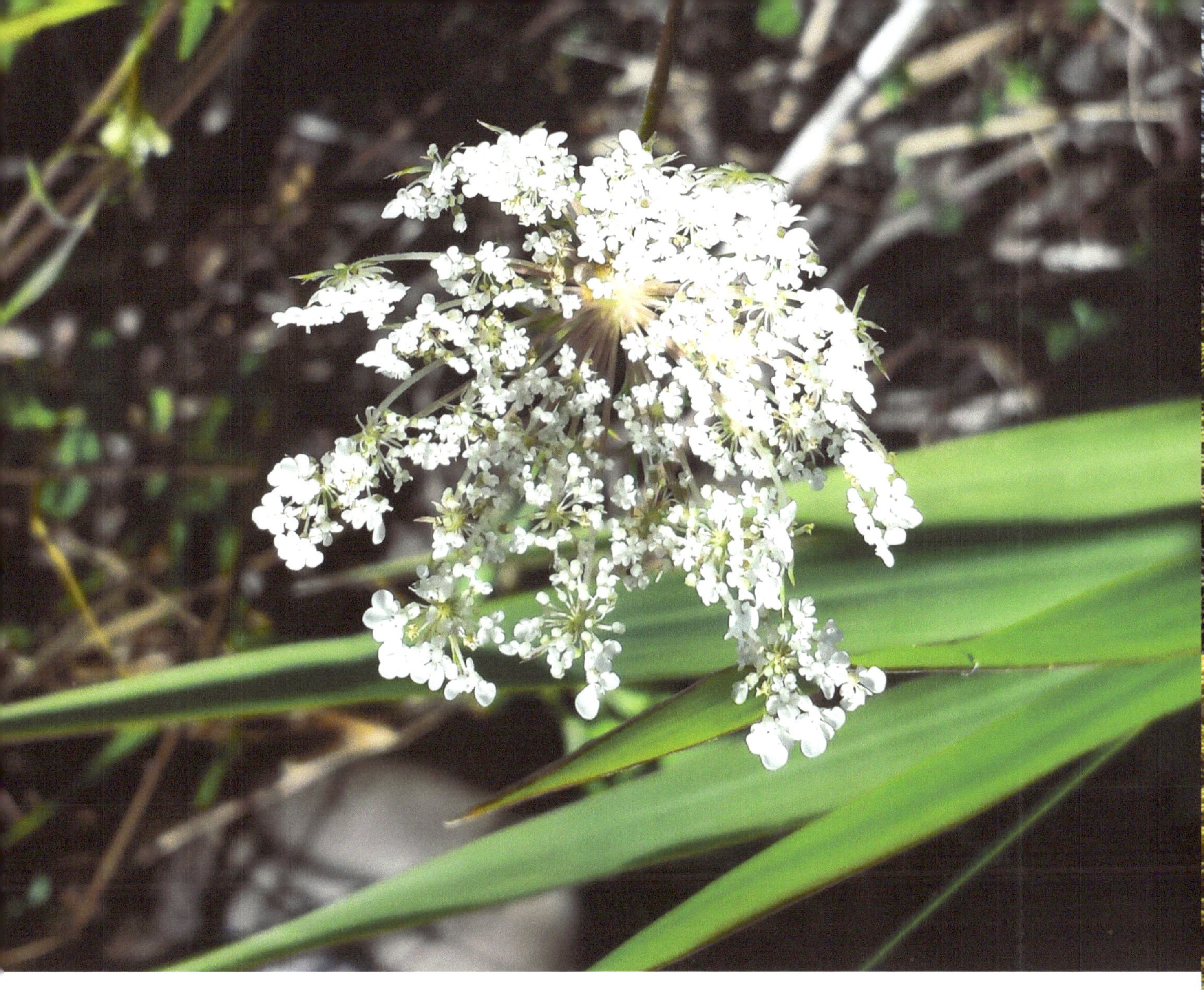

No mordant
Alum, pH 7
Alum, pH 4
Alum, pH 10
Alum & iron

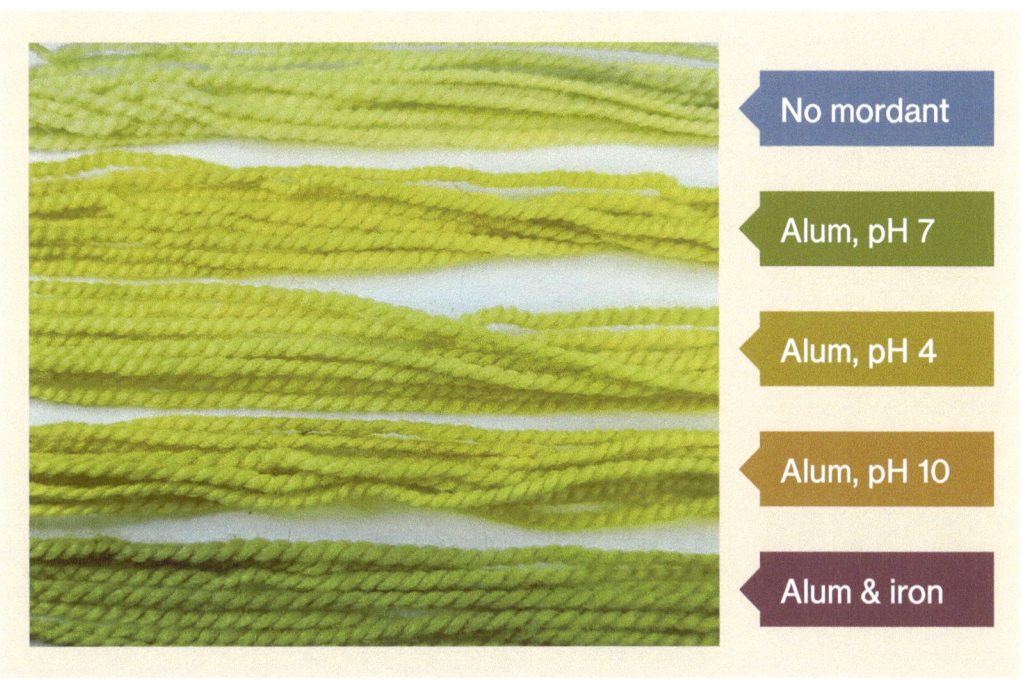

NOTES

SIBERIAN PEASHRUB

(Caragana arborescens)

As the name implies, Siberian peashrub is native to Siberia and northern China. It is a pea family member, and the seeds have been used as food for both humans and chickens. It was brought to North America by immigrants in the 1800s for use as food and windbreaks. It is a tall shrub or small tree, reaching up to 20 feet (6 m) with grey bark. The leaves are compound with individual leaflets coming off the central stem in pairs. Each leaflet is oval with a smooth edge. The stems arise singly from nodes along the branches. Yellow, pea-type flowers appear in the early spring. The flowers are small, sweetly fragrant, and grow from stalks at the leaf node. They attract bees. The seedpods which form are roughly 2 inches (5cm) long and round. Inside are up to 6 small yellow to brown "peas." When mature, the pod splits and curls, releasing the seeds. The roots form a broad, dense network, so it has been planted for erosion control. As a pea family member, the roots contain small nodules filled with bacteria that pull nitrogen gas from the air and "fix" it, converting the nitrogen to a form usable by the plant.

The Siberian pea shrub can tolerate harsh conditions. Its ability to make its own fertilizer gives it a competitive advantage over native plants. It grows rapidly and can colonize grasslands, displacing native species.

When Siberian peashrub invades prairies, controlled burns can be used to remove it. However, it can sprout from the roots, so additional burns or physically removing the sprouts may be necessary. Seedlings can be pulled.

The leaves and flowers of Siberian peashrub produce yellow to greenish brown results on wool. Simmer the leaves and flowers with water for 30 minutes, then strain. Add the fiber and any modifiers and continue simmering for 30 minutes. Allow to cool in the pot overnight.

Some references say a blue dye can be obtained from the leaves but give no instructions. Indigo is also a member of the pea family. Attempts to treat peashrub like indigo to produce blue have been unsuccessful to date. However, experimentation is encouraged.

Spotted Knapweed

(Centaurea stoebe)
(Centaurea maculosa)

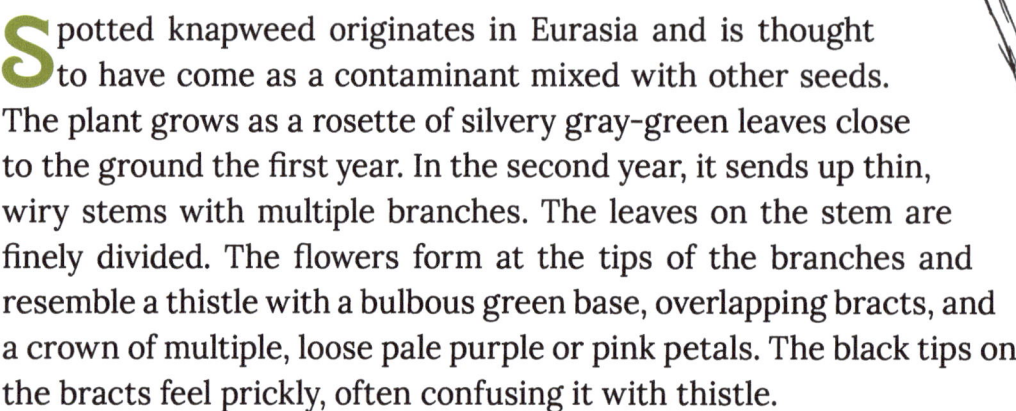

Spotted knapweed originates in Eurasia and is thought to have come as a contaminant mixed with other seeds. The plant grows as a rosette of silvery gray-green leaves close to the ground the first year. In the second year, it sends up thin, wiry stems with multiple branches. The leaves on the stem are finely divided. The flowers form at the tips of the branches and resemble a thistle with a bulbous green base, overlapping bracts, and a crown of multiple, loose pale purple or pink petals. The black tips on the bracts feel prickly, often confusing it with thistle.

Spotted knapweed invades fields, roadsides, and waste ground. It tolerates dry and sandy soils, outcompeting other native plants. It is reported to be allelopathic, secreting chemicals from the roots which inhibit other plants. This allows it to create monocultures that are not eaten by most grazers. In ranching areas, this decreases the food available to cattle.

Mowing before seed set is one method of preventing the spread of spotted knapweed. The plants can be pulled or dug, but they can regrow if fragments of the long taproot remain in the ground. Biological controls in the form of weevils are being used to kill the plant by attacking both the roots and the seed head.

Knapweed dyes wool shades of yellow to gold. The entire plant is used. Increasing the ratio of plant material to fiber produces deeper shades. Cover the plant material with water and simmer for up to an hour. Strain the dye and add the fiber and any modifiers. Simmer for an hour and allow the fiber to cool in the dye bath overnight. The addition of iron as a modifier shifts the color to gray.

TANSY

(Tanacetum vulgare)

Tansy is a perennial weed found growing throughout North America, as well as its native Asia and Europe. It thrives in disturbed ground, both wet and dry, and can form large monocultures, shading out other plants and creating a tangled mat of fibrous roots. Tansy plants grow with a single, unbranched stem, reaching up to 4 feet (approximately 1.2 meters). The leaves are pinnately compound, up to 10 inches (25 cm) long, with many heavily toothed leaflets. They appear almost fern-like. Bright yellow flowers appear at the top of the plant on small branches in clusters of dime-sized flowerheads, giving the plant another of its common names, yellow buttons. The entire plant gives off a strong, pungent odor someplace between camphor and mint. Tansy is herbaceous, dying back to the ground each fall and regrowing from the roots each spring. Large stands of the dry, dark brown stems remain standing most of the winter, shedding seeds and providing both food and shelter to wildlife.

Tansy has a long history of uses. Young spring leaves have been used as a seasoning, similar to sage, but more bitter. However, the mature plant produces an oil that is toxic to many insects, humans, and many livestock. It can produce contact dermatitis in insensitive individuals. Tansy can produce seizures when ingested. In the past, tansy tea was used to induce abortions. The pungent scent of the plant is thought to repel cloth moths, which is why it is often mixed with cedar to repel them.

The large, spreading rhizome mass and thousands of seeds produced by the flowerheads contribute to the invasiveness of the plant. In addition, few animals besides goats and grasshoppers graze the plant. This lack of predation also contributes to the plant's invasiveness. Methods to control tansy involve removing the flowerheads before they set seed

and mowing large stands to prevent reseeding. These methods do not prevent regrowth from the roots. Preventing light from reaching the roots with mulches prevents regrowth. A more labor-intensive method is actually digging out the roots. Neither mulch nor digging is practical on large growths.

The leaves and flowers of tansy produce dyes ranging from yellows to green. Simmer the chopped plant material with water to cover. Keep the temperature at a low simmer; boiling turns the dye brown. After about an hour, filter the dye and add your fibers to the liquid. Simmer together for 30 minutes to an hour. If using a modifier, add it now. Acids shift the color to more yellow, whereas adding a base brings out a more golden/bronze color. Iron shifts the color to an olive green. Allow the fibers to cool in the bath overnight for the deepest shades.

- No mordant
- Alum, pH 7
- Alum, pH 4
- Alum, pH 10
- Alum & iron

WOAD

(Isatis tinctoria)

Dyeing with woad is a somewhat magical process, *unlike other dye processes.* Woad is a northern European species that produces the same blue pigment, indigotin, the subtropical species indigo, though in less quantities. There are few natural sources of blue dyes, so the fact that woad would grow in northern North America made it very popular with early settlers. The dye does not require a mordant and will adhere to animal and plant fibers. In addition to its use as a dye, woad has been used medicinally. Even today, it is being explored for its antiviral, antibacterial, and antitumor properties.

The plant is a biennial. In the first year, it grows a rosette of elongated, lance-like leaves with a slightly rippled edge. The leaves have a bluish-green color. The rosette lies close to the ground. It is these first-year leaves that produce the blue pigment. In the second year, the plant sends up a tall flower stalk approximately 3 feet (1 meter), topped with multiple tiny branches full of 4-petaled, yellow flowers. These give way to dangling seeds.

A single woad plant can produce almost 100 seeds. The seeds are slightly barbed, sticking to both clothing and fur. The plants often form monocultures, shading out native species. It is considered invasive in rangeland areas. Control involves the removal of the seed heads to prevent dispersal

The traditional process of producing blue dye involves fermenting first-year leaves, harvested mid to late summer, in an oxygen-free environment and then adding an alkali, traditionally chalk and stale urine. Today, washing soda is often used. However, there are numerous methods of extracting the pigment. **On the next page,** you will find one of the simpler methods that takes advantage of modern chemicals. Make sure to wear gloves and work in a well-ventilated area or wear a respirator.

WOAD *(Continued)*

WOAD DYING PROCESS

1 — Create an initial extraction by tearing up about a pound of fresh leaves and pouring boiling water over them to cover. Let them steep until cool.

2 — Drain off the dye liquid and squeeze the leaves well to get every bit of dye. The liquid should be reddish brown.

3 — Heat the liquid to hot, but not yet simmering, around 120 F (50 C). Remove from the heat.

4 — Gently stir in enough washing soda (sodium carbonate) to shift the color to slightly greenish.

5 — Once the color has shifted, begin incorporating air by whisking vigorously. A blue froth should begin to form on the surface.

| 6 | Reheat to 120 F and gently stir in about 1/8th cup of color run remover (thiourea dioxide). This removes oxygen from your liquid. |

| 7 | Remove from the heat and allow to cool for several hours. Do not stir. The liquid should shift color to yellow-green. |

| 8 | Carefully add wet fiber to the dye liquid to avoid adding air. |

| 9 | Allow the fiber to soak for 15 to 20 minutes, carefully moving it once or twice. |

| 10 | Remove the fiber, being careful not to allow drips into the dye bath. The fiber will be greenish. |

| 11 | Hang the fiber and watch as the color shifts to blue. |

| 12 | Allow the fiber to dry fully before rinsing. |

WORMWOOD

(Artemisia absinthium)

Mention wormwood and many people think of absinthe, the potent alcoholic beverage with a dark history. Wormwood is a perennial plant native to southern Eurasia and parts of northern Africa. It spread throughout Europe and into North America due to its use as a garden plant, an insecticide, and its medicinal properties. Wormwood grows in sandy soils, sending out a fibrous root system that helps prevent it from being eroded and helps it gather water. It reaches a height of up to 3 feet (1 meter) and has a central stem with multiple branches. Small yellow flowers form on the upper branches. The leaves are finely divided, larger at the plant's base, and covered with down and oil glands. The silvery gray-green foliage is prized by gardeners, and a number of noninvasive cultivars have been developed for the landscape industry. Both insects and most wildlife avoid eating it due to its bitter flavor.

Yet that bitterness is why it is incorporated into alcoholic beverages, absinthe being the most known. Small amounts are also used in a number of bitters formulas. The oils it produces are reported to repel insects, and branches are sometimes incorporated into animal bedding and herbal insect-repellant bags. It has been used medicinally throughout history for treating fevers and expelling parasites, as well as fungal infections. Modern medicine is exploring its use in malaria treatment and for digestive disorders.

Wormwood can become invasive due to its ability to survive in poor, dry soils. It grows rapidly and produces large numbers of seeds. The bitterness and oils it produces discourage grazing by most animals, giving it an advantage over native plants. The dense growth can shade out other plants.

The habit of growing in sandy soils makes it easier to pull plants. Clipping the flower heads before the seeds set controls its spread. Gardeners are encouraged to plant the noninvasive cultivars.

The entire plant is used for dyeing. Simmer fresh leaves with enough water to cover for about 30 minutes. Strain the liquid and add the prepared fiber. Simmer for another 30 minutes. Add any modifiers, if desired, and allow the fiber to cool in the bath overnight. Wormwood produces soft yellows under most conditions, though adding iron shifts the color to a sage green.

NOTES

ABOUT THE AUTHOR

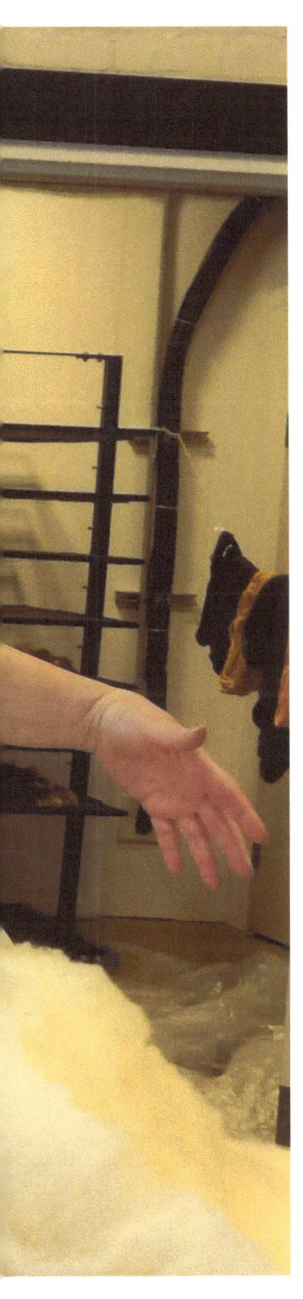

Theresa Hornstein is a biologist and fiber artist who blends science with creativity in unexpected ways. With 35 years of teaching under her belt—15 of those focused on fiber arts—she brings a hands-on, curiosity-driven approach to every class, encouraging experimentation over perfection. Her passion lies in transforming invasive species into stunning natural dyes, using each project as a chance to explore, learn, and connect. Whether in a classroom, at a workshop, or crafting on the go, Theresa sparks conversations through the vivid colors of her work. This book captures her unique perspective, inviting readers into the rich intersection of biology, art, and storytelling.

If you're interested in bringing Theresa to speak or teach for your group, she'd love to connect.

Reach out at *greylady32@yahoo.com*.